Traditional
HOT PUDDINGS

by Sue Ashworth
Illustrated by Julia Bigg

First published in Great Britain in 1994 by
Parragon Book Service Ltd
Unit 13–17
Avonbridge Trading Estate
Atlantic Road
Avonmouth
Bristol BS11 9QD

ISBN 1 85813 698 9

Edited, designed and typeset by Haldane Mason
Editor: Joanna Swinnerton

Printed in Italy

Note: Cup measurements in this book are for American cups. Tablespoons are assumed to be 15ml.
Unless otherwise stated, milk is assumed to be full-fat and eggs are standard size 2.

CONTENTS

BREAD AND BUTTER PUDDING

SERVES ❹

60 g/2 oz/¼ cup butter, softened

6 thin slices bread, crusts removed

60 g/2 oz/⅓ cup sultanas (golden raisins), raisins or currants

150 ml/¼ pint/⅔ cup single (light) cream

300 ml/½ pint/1¼ cups milk

30 g/1 oz/2 tbsp light muscovado or caster (superfine) sugar

2 large eggs, beaten

½ tsp vanilla flavouring (extract)

pinch of ground nutmeg (freshly ground if possible)

A true nursery pudding – everyone seems to have childhood memories of this dessert. A more sophisticated version can be made by adding a couple of tablespoons of sherry to the milk mixture.

1 Grease a shallow baking dish with some of the butter.

2 Spread the rest of the butter on the slices of bread. Cut them into triangles and arrange them in layers, buttered side up, in the dish. Scatter the sultanas (golden raisins), raisins or currants over the top.

3 Put the cream, milk and sugar into a saucepan and heat gently until the sugar has dissolved, but do not allow the mixture to get too hot. Whisk the eggs and vanilla flavouring (extract) together, then add the cream mixture, whisking constantly. Pour over the bread through a sieve (strainer) and allow to soak for at least 1 hour.

4 Sprinkle the surface of the pudding with ground nutmeg. Stand the baking dish in

a shallow tin (pan) of warm water, such as a roasting tin (pan), and place in a preheated oven at 180°C, 350°F, Gas Mark 4. Bake for 30–40 minutes, until set and golden brown.

GOLDEN SYRUP SPONGE

A traditional steamed syrup sponge pudding is hearty, welcoming food, just right served on a cold winter's day. You can reduce the cooking time by microwaving the pudding on full power for 3½–4 minutes, then leaving it for 4–5 minutes to complete the cooking process before serving.

SERVES 4

75 ml/3 fl oz/⅓ cup plus 1 tbsp golden (light corn) syrup

90 g/3 oz/⅓ cup butter or margarine

90 g/3 oz/½ cup light muscovado sugar

1 egg, beaten

175 g/6 oz/1½ cups self-raising flour

pinch of salt

2–3 tbsp milk

custard sauce to serve

1 Grease a 1.25 litre/ 2¼ pint/5 cup pudding basin with a little butter. Spoon in the syrup, spreading some of it around the sides of the basin.

2 Cream the butter and sugar together until light and fluffy, then add the egg a little at a time, beating well between each addition. Sift the flour and salt together, then fold into the mixture using a large metal spoon. Add a little milk until the mixture reaches a soft, dropping consistency. Spoon into the pudding basin and level the surface.

3 Butter a piece of greaseproof paper (baking parchment) and make a 2.5 cm/1 inch pleat down the centre to allow the pudding to expand. Place over the pudding, buttered side down, and secure around the basin with string. Place in a steamer set over a large saucepan of steadily boiling water, and steam for 2½ hours, topping up with boiling water when necessary. Keep a

close eye on the saucepan and
never allow it to boil dry.

When cooked, turn the
pudding out on to a hot plate
and serve with custard sauce.

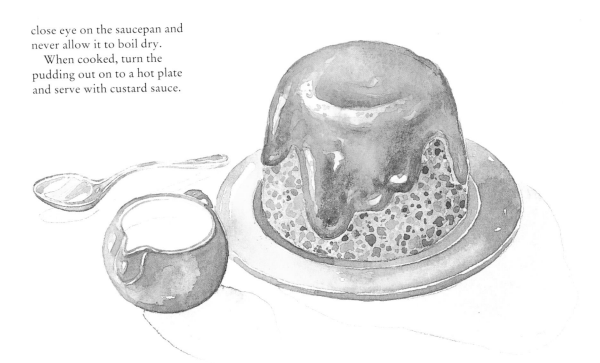

LATTICE-TOPPED TREACLE TART

This treacle – or, rather, golden (light corn) syrup – tart is a real rib-sticking treat, perfect served on a cold winter's day with a jug of custard.

1 Sift the flour and salt into a large mixing bowl. Cut the butter and lard (shortening) into pieces and add to the bowl. Rub in with your fingertips until the mixture resembles fine breadcrumbs. Add enough chilled water to make a firm dough. Knead lightly for a few moments, wrap in clingfilm (plastic wrap) and refrigerate for 10 minutes.

2 Roll out three quarters of the dough on a lightly floured work surface (counter) and use to line a 17 cm/7 inch metal pie plate.

3 Warm the syrup slightly and mix in the breadcrumbs and lemon rind. Spoon into the tart. Roll out the remaining dough and cut into narrow strips. Interweave them to make a lattice top for the tart.

4 Place in a preheated oven at 220°C, 425°F, Gas Mark 7

and bake for about 20 minutes until golden brown. Serve with custard or cream.

Transfer to the baking dish.
the ingredients are combined.
middle, pour in the
melted butter mixture
and stir well so that all
make a well in the
a large bowl and
salt together

10

STICKY TOFFEE PUDDING

This is one of those wonderful puddings of which everyone can manage to eat just a little bit more, no matter how much you make, or how often.

SERVES 4

175 g/6 oz/¾ cup butter or margarine

175 g/6 oz/¾ cup dark muscovado sugar

2 tbsp golden (light corn) syrup

2 eggs, beaten

125 g/4 oz/1 cup self-raising flour

pinch of salt

whipped cream to serve

1 Grease a 1.25 litre/2¼ pint/5 cup ovenproof dish.

2 Put 60 g/2 oz/¼ cup of the butter, 60 g/2 oz/⅓ cup of the sugar and the golden (light corn) syrup into a saucepan. Heat very gently to melt the butter and dissolve the sugar. Pour into the base of the greased baking dish.

3 Put the remaining butter and sugar in the saucepan and heat very gently to melt the butter, but do not allow it to get too hot. Remove from the heat and cool slightly, then add the beaten eggs, mixing well.

4 Sift the fl and

5 Place in a preheated oven at 180°C, 350°F, Gas Mark 4, and bake for 40–45 minutes until firm and springy to the touch. Turn out on to a hot plate, and serve accompanied by some fresh whipped cream.

BAKEWELL PUDDINGS

A lovely, light almond filling covers a layer of raspberry or strawberry jam (preserves) in these puff pastry tarts or 'puddings', as they are traditionally called.

SERVES ❹

175 g/6 oz frozen puff pastry, defrosted

2–3 tbsp raspberry or strawberry jam (preserves)

90 g/3 oz/⅓ cup butter, softened

90 g/3 oz/⅓ cup caster (superfine) sugar

2 eggs, beaten

90 g/3 oz/¾ cup ground almonds

single (light) cream or custard sauce to serve

1 Roll out the pastry dough on a lightly floured work surface (counter) and use to line 6 Yorkshire pudding tins (pans) or muffin tins (pans), trimming the dough close to the edge. (If preferred, line a 20 cm/8 inch deep metal pie plate with the dough.) Spread the jam (preserves) over the base of the pastry dough cases.

2 Cream the butter and sugar together until light and fluffy, then add the beaten egg gradually, beating well between each addition. Mix in the ground almonds. Spoon into the cases and spread out evenly to cover the jam (preserves).

3 Place in a preheated oven at 200°C, 400°F, Gas Mark 6, and bake for 20–25 minutes until

the filling is set and the pastry is
cooked and golden brown. Serve
hot with single (light) cream or
custard sauce.

SAUCY LEMON LAYER PUDDING

An airy sponge layer forms on the top of this simple-to-make pudding with its lovely lemon sauce beneath.

SERVES ❹

60 g/2 oz/¼ cup butter or margarine

125 g/4 oz/½ cup caster (superfine) sugar

finely grated rind of 1 large lemon

3 eggs, separated

90 g/3 oz/¾ cup self-raising flour

300 ml/½ pint/1¼ cups milk

75 ml/3 fl oz/⅓ cup lemon juice

1 Grease a 1.25 litre/2¼ pint ovenproof dish with a little of the butter or margarine.

2 Cream the remaining butter or margarine with the sugar until light and fluffy, then add the lemon rind. Add the egg yolks one at a time, beating well between each addition.

3 Fold the flour into the mixture using a large metal spoon, then stir in the milk and lemon juice. At this stage the batter will be quite thin and will look slightly curdled.

4 Whisk the egg whites until stiff, but not dry, then fold into the lemon batter with the large metal spoon.

5 Pour the mixture into the greased dish and stand the dish in a shallow tin (pan) of warm water, such as a roasting tin (pan). Place in a preheated oven at 190°C, 375°F, Gas Mark 5, and bake for about 50 minutes until well risen and golden brown.

APPLE CHARLOTTE

If you don't possess a charlotte mould (and not many of us do), use a soufflé dish or deep-sided baking dish instead. The results will taste every bit as good.

1 Put the apples, brown sugar and 30 g/1 oz/2 tbsp of the butter into a saucepan with the lemon rind, lemon juice and mixed (apple pie) spice. Simmer gently for about 10 minutes, until soft and pulpy. Remove from the heat.

2 Cut each slice of bread into 3 strips, and fry them in the remaining butter and oil until golden brown and crisp. Lift them out as they cook, and drain on paper towels. Reserve some of the strips and use the rest to line the base and sides of a 900 ml/1½ pint/3½ cup soufflé dish or charlotte mould. Spoon in the cooked apple mixture and level the surface. Arrange the reserved strips of bread over the top and

sprinkle with half the caster (superfine) sugar. Place in a preheated oven at 200°C, 400°F, Gas Mark 6, and bake for about 20 minutes. Turn out on to a hot plate and sprinkle with the remaining sugar. Serve hot with custard sauce or cream.

RASPBERRY AND COCONUT ROLY POLY

Simple and satisfying, baked jam roly poly is sprinkled with desiccated (shredded) coconut to give it a lovely flavour. This is a favourite with kids – no matter what their age!

SERVES 6

175 g/6 oz/1½ cups self-raising flour

pinch of salt

90 g/3 oz/generous ½ cup shredded suet

250 g/8 oz/¾ cup raspberry jam (preserves)

60 g/2 oz/⅔ cup desiccated (shredded) coconut

custard sauce to serve

1 Sift the flour and salt into a large mixing bowl and add the suet, stirring to mix. Add sufficient chilled water to give a soft, but not sticky, dough. Turn the dough out on to a lightly floured work surface (counter) and roll out to form a rectangle measuring about 30 x 25 cm (12 x 10 inches).

2 Spread the jam (preserves) over the dough to within 2.5 cm/1 inch of the sides. Sprinkle the coconut over the top. Moisten the edges of the dough with water and roll up from the shortest edge, pinching the edges together to seal them. Lift on to a lightly oiled baking sheet, positioning the roll so that the seam is underneath.

3 Place in a preheated oven at 220°C/425°F/Gas Mark 7, and bake for 20 minutes, then reduce the temperature to 200°C/400°F/ Gas Mark 6 and bake for a further 20 minutes until golden brown.

Serve with custard sauce.

CHOCOLATE CASTLE PUDDINGS WITH RICH CHOCOLATE SAUCE

For confirmed chocoholics, these puddings offer no help for those who want to kick the habit. They are just too delicious for words!

1 Grease 4 dariole moulds (muffin cups) or individual pudding basins with butter.

2 Cream the butter or margarine and sugar together until light and fluffy. Add the egg gradually, beating well between each addition. Fold in the flour using a large metal spoon, then stir in the melted chocolate, mixing well. Divide the mixture between the prepared moulds to fill them about two thirds from the top. Cover each one tightly with a piece of foil.

3 Place in a steamer set over a saucepan of gently boiling water and steam for 40 minutes. Top up with boiling water as necessary. Do not allow the pan to boil dry.

4 To make the sauce, put the cocoa, cornflour

20

SPOTTED DICK

As this traditional suet pudding steams slowly, the air fills with the citrus smell of lemon rind, which gives the dessert a delicious flavour.

SERVES 4

90 g/3 oz/¾ cup self-raising flour

pinch of salt

90 g/3 oz/1½ cups fresh white breadcrumbs

90 g/3 oz/scant ½ cup shredded suet

175 g/6 oz/1 cup currants

90 g/3 oz/½ cup light muscovado sugar

finely grated rind of 1 large lemon

about 75 ml/3 fl oz/⅓ cup milk

custard or lemon-flavoured sauce to serve

1 Sift the flour and salt into a large bowl and stir in the breadcrumbs, suet, currants, sugar and half the lemon rind. Add sufficient milk to make a fairly soft dough, mixing with a round-bladed knife.

2 Knead gently for a few seconds on a lightly floured work surface (counter) and form into a roll about 15 cm/6 inches long.

Wrap loosely in greased greaseproof paper (baking parchment), wrap in foil and seal the ends well.

3 Place in a steamer set over a pan of boiling water and steam for 1½ hours. Top up with boiling water when necessary to prevent the pan from boiling dry.

4 Serve the pudding with custard or a sweet white sauce flavoured with the remaining lemon rind.

24

SPICED APPLE PIE

A generous filling of sliced apples, cooked in butter and brown sugar, then dusted with cinnamon, gives a classic apple pie a heavenly flavour. Serve hot with real dairy ice cream.

SERVES 4

250 g/8 oz/2 cups plain (all-purpose) flour

pinch of salt

175 g/6 oz/¾ cup butter, chilled

500g/1 lb cooking apples, peeled, cored and thinly sliced

60 g/2 oz/⅓ cup soft brown sugar

½ tsp ground cinnamon

2 tbsp water

1 tbsp cornflour (cornstarch)

1 tbsp milk for glazing

1 Sift the flour and salt into a large mixing bowl. Cut 125 g/4 oz/½ cup of the butter into pieces, add to the flour and rub in with your fingertips until it resembles fine breadcrumbs. Stir in enough chilled water to make a firm dough. Knead lightly for a few moments, then wrap in clingfilm (plastic wrap) and chill for about 10 minutes.

2 Melt the remaining butter in a large frying pan (skillet) and fry the apples gently for 3–4 minutes. Remove from the heat and stir in the sugar, cinnamon and water, mixing well. Sprinkle with the cornflour (cornstarch) and stir well to blend. Allow the mixture to cool.

3 Roll out half the dough on a lightly floured work surface (counter) and use to line a 20cm/8 inch metal pie plate. Spoon in the filling. Roll out the rest of the dough, moisten the edges and position over

the filling, pressing the edges together to seal them. Trim the edges and use any remaining dough to make leaves to decorate the top.

4 Brush the top with milk. Place in a preheated oven at 200°C, 400°F, Gas Mark 6, and bake for 35–40 minutes.

QUEEN OF PUDDINGS

It's no wonder that this dessert has earned its royal title, with its delicious light breadcrumb base, topped with a golden crown of meringue.

1 Grease a 1.25 litre/2¼ pint/ 5 cup baking dish with a little of the butter. Scatter the breadcrumbs in the base of the dish.

2 Put the remaining butter into a saucepan with the milk, lemon rind and half the sugar. Cook gently over a low heat until lukewarm, then remove from the heat and beat in the egg yolks. Pour through a sieve (strainer) into the baking dish and allow to stand (sit) for 20–30 minutes.

3 Place in a preheated oven at 180°C, 350°F, Gas Mark 4, and bake for 25–30 minutes until set. Remove from the oven and spread the jam (preserves) over the surface. Whisk the egg whites in a grease-free bowl until stiff, but not dry. Add the remaining sugar and

28

whisk until glossy. Pile on top of the pudding, decorate with cherries and angelica, and bake for a further 10–15 minutes until light golden brown.

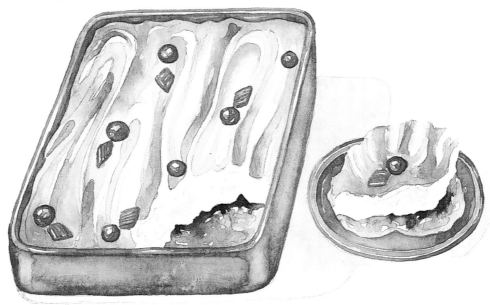

CHERRY BATTER PUDDING

This pudding is best made when fresh black cherries are plentiful and full of flavour. However, you can use well-drained canned black cherries if no fresh ones are available.

1 Grease a shallow 1.25 litre/2¼ pint/5 cup ovenproof dish with vegetable oil. Scatter the cherries evenly across the base.

2 Sift the flour and salt into a large mixing bowl. Add the egg yolk, milk and caster (superfine) sugar and beat together with a balloon whisk until smooth. Whip the egg white in a grease-free bowl (using a clean whisk) until stiff, but not dry. Fold into the batter mixture with a large metal spoon.

3 Pour into the baking dish and place immediately in a preheated oven at 200°C, 400°F, Gas Mark 6. Bake for 25–30 minutes until risen and golden brown. Serve sprinkled with the icing (confectioners') sugar.

PAN-COOKED TOFFEE BREAD

This is the perfect dessert to make when you want something quick and economical to round off a mid-week meal.

1 Beat the eggs, milk and cinnamon together in a shallow bowl. Cut the bread into triangles and soak them in the egg and milk mixture, a few at a time, until the mixture has been absorbed.

2 Melt 60 g/2 oz/¼ cup of the butter in a large frying pan (skillet) with a few drops of oil to prevent the butter from burning. Fry the bread triangles until they are golden brown, turning them over to cook on the other side. Add a little extra butter and vegetable oil to the frying pan (skillet) as required. Lift out the cooked bread triangles and keep warm on 4 hot serving plates.

3 Add the rest of the butter to the pan with the sugar and syrup and heat until melted and bubbling. Pour over the bread triangles and serve at once.

TRADITIONAL RICE PUDDING

A rice pudding is no trouble at all to make, and cooks gently to make a comforting, creamy-rich dessert. Use full-cream milk for the best flavour – long-life milk works particularly well.

SERVES ❹

45 g/1½ oz/generous 3 tbsp short-grain rice, rinsed with cold water

30 g/1 oz/2 tbsp butter

45 g/1½ oz/3 tbsp sugar

generous pinch of ground nutmeg (freshly ground, if possible)

pinch of salt

600 ml/1 pint/2½ cups full-cream milk, preferably long-life

1 Sprinkle the rice in a 1.25 litre/2¼ pint/5 cup deep ovenproof dish. Add just enough cold water to cover the rice.

2 Place in a preheated oven at 180°C, 350°F, Gas Mark 4, and bake for about 20 minutes until the rice has absorbed the water. Remove the dish from the oven.

3 Add the butter to the baking dish, using a knife to run it around the sides of the dish to grease it. (This also helps to prevent the pudding from boiling over). Add the sugar, nutmeg and salt, stirring to mix well. Pour in the milk and stir.

34

Sprinkle a little extra nutmeg over the surface.

4 Return the dish to the oven, reduce the temperature to 150°C, 300°F, Gas Mark 2, and bake for about 2 hours.

CHRISTMAS PUDDING

A moist pudding with a full mature flavour is made by soaking the ingredients in brandy (or rum if you prefer). Long, slow steaming also guarantees a delicious, mellow pudding. This pudding can be stored for up to 4 months.

SERVES ❻

500 g/1 lb/3 cups seedless raisins

250 g/8 oz/1¼ cups currants

60 g/2 oz/¼ cup glacé (candied) cherries, halved

1 large carrot, grated finely

1 dessert apple, grated finely

125 g/4 oz/⅔ cup molasses sugar

125 g/4 oz/1 cup ground almonds

125 g/4 oz/2 cups wholemeal (whole wheat) breadcrumbs

1 tsp ground mixed spice (apple pie spice)

freshly grated rind of 1 lemon

4 tbsp lemon juice

150 ml/¼ pint/⅔ cup brandy

15g/½ oz/1 tbsp butter

2 eggs, beaten

1 Put all the ingredients except for the butter and eggs in a large mixing bowl and stir well. Cover and leave in a cool place for at least 6–8 hours.

2 Grease a 1.25 litre/2¼ pint/ 5 cup pudding basin with the butter. Add the eggs to the other ingredients, stirring well to incorporate thoroughly. Spoon the mixture into the basin and place a circle of buttered greaseproof paper (baking parchment) on the surface. Cover the basin with greaseproof paper (baking parchment) and a pudding cloth or a piece of foil, and secure with string.

3 Place in a steamer set over a saucepan of steadily boiling water and steam for 6 hours. Top up with boiling water

36

when necessary. Never allow the saucepan to boil dry. When cooked, leave to cool, then cover with a fresh piece of greaseproof paper (baking parchment), foil or cloth and store in a cool place. Steam for 3 hours to reheat on Christmas Day.

RHUBARB AND GINGER CRUMBLE

A little chopped stem (candied) ginger gives an interesting lift to a favourite farmhouse-style pudding. Vanilla ice cream makes the perfect accompaniment.

1 Put the rhubarb into a 1.25 litre/2¼ pint/5 cup ovenproof dish and add the chopped stem (candied) ginger and granulated sugar, stirring to mix. Sprinkle with the water.

2 Sift the flour, salt and ground ginger into a large mixing bowl. Cut the butter or margarine into small pieces and add to the flour. Rub in with your fingertips until the mixture resembles fine breadcrumbs. Stir in the rolled oats and demerara sugar (coffee crystals). Scatter this mixture evenly over the fruit to cover it completely.

3 Place in a preheated oven at 180°C, 350°F, Gas Mark 4, and bake for 40–45 minutes until golden brown on top.

GOOSEBERRY COBBLER

500 g/1 lb/2½ cups gooseberries, topped and tailed

125 g/4 oz/½ cup sugar

250 g/8 oz/2 cups self-raising flour

pinch of salt

60 g/2 oz/¼ cup butter or margarine, chilled

about 150 ml/¼ pint/⅔ cup milk

'Cobbler' is the name for a scone topping, placed in circles around the edge of a baking dish. Gooseberries are used to great effect here, but you could use apples, rhubarb, apricots or plums as an alternative.

1 Put the gooseberries with a little water and 90 g/3 oz/⅓ cup of the sugar into a saucepan and simmer until just cooked.

2 Grease a 1.25 litre/2¼ pint/5 cup ovenproof dish with a little butter and spoon the fruit into the base.

3 Sift the flour and salt into a large mixing bowl. Cut the butter or margarine into pieces and add to the flour, then rub in with your fingertips until the mixture resembles fine breadcrumbs. Stir in the remaining sugar and add sufficient milk to give a soft, but not sticky, dough.

4 Turn the dough out on to a lightly floured work surface (counter) and roll out to a thickness of 1 cm/½ inch. Cut the dough into rounds, using a 4 cm/1½ inch cutter, and place them around the edge of the dish, overlapping them to fit. Brush with a little milk to glaze.

Place in a preheated oven at
220°C, 425°F, Gas Mark 7, and
bake for 10–15 minutes, until the
cobbler topping has risen and is
golden brown.

PINEAPPLE AND CHERRY UPSIDE-DOWN PUDDING

Pineapple rings and glacé (candied) cherries are arranged in the base of a baking dish and covered with sponge. When the pudding is turned out, the fruit makes an attractive jewelled topping. Serve with a sauce made from the pineapple juice, or with custard.

SERVES ❹

1 tsp butter

2 tbsp golden (light corn) syrup, warmed

250 g/8 oz can pineapple rings in natural juice

a few glacé (candied) cherries

125 g/4 oz/½ cup butter

125 g/4 oz/½ cup golden caster (superfine) sugar

2 eggs, beaten

175 g/6 oz/1½ cups self-raising flour

2–3 tbsp milk

2 tsp cornflour (cornstarch), blended with a little cold water

1 Grease an 18 cm/7 inch round baking dish or cake tin (pan) with the teaspoonful of butter. Spoon in the syrup and spread over the base.

2 Drain the pineapple rings, reserving the juice. Reserve one pineapple ring and cut all the others in half. Place the whole ring in the centre of the baking dish or cake tin (pan) and arrange the cut halves around it. Put a glacé (candied) cherry into the middle of each piece of pineapple.

3 Cream the butter and sugar together until light and fluffy, then add the beaten eggs a little at a time, beating well between each addition. Fold in the flour using a large metal spoon, adding enough milk to give the mixture a soft, dropping consistency. Spread over the pineapples and cherries.

4 Place in a preheated oven at 180°C, 350°F, Gas Mark 4, and bake for about 45 minutes until springy to the touch.

42

5 To make the pineapple sauce, mix the reserved pineapple juice with the blended cornflour (cornstarch). Cook over a low heat, stirring constantly, until the sauce is thickened and smooth. Turn out the pudding and serve with the sauce.

APRICOT AND BANANA MERINGUE

SERVES ❹

475 g/15 oz can apricots in natural juice

2 bananas, sliced

150 ml/¼ pint/⅔ cup single (light) cream

2 eggs, separated

1 tbsp cornflour (cornstarch)

60 g/2 oz/¼ cup caster (superfine) sugar

Canned apricots and sliced bananas are combined in a creamy sauce made from the apricot juice, single (light) cream and egg yolks. Topped with golden-brown meringue, this makes a delicious dessert.

1 Grease a 1.25 litre/2¼ pint/5 cup ovenproof dish with a little butter.

2 Drain the apricot juice into a small saucepan and put the apricots into the ovenproof dish with the sliced bananas, stirring to combine.

3 Put the cream, egg yolks, cornflour (cornstarch) and 30 g/1 oz/2 tbsp of the sugar into the saucepan with the apricot juice and stir together using a small balloon whisk. Cook over a gentle heat, stirring constantly, until thickened and blended. Pour into the baking dish and mix with the fruit. Place in a preheated oven at 190°C, 375°F, Gas Mark 5, and cook for 5 minutes while making the meringue topping.

4 Whisk the egg whites (using a clean whisk) in a large grease-free bowl until stiff but not dry. Add the remaining sugar and whisk again until glossy. Remove the baking dish from the oven and pile the

44

meringue on top of the pudding. Return to the oven and bake for about 15 minutes until golden brown.

FRUIT FRITTERS WITH BUTTERSCOTCH SAUCE

These irresistible banana, apple and pineapple fritters are drizzled with warm syrup and sprinkled with toasted sesame seeds

SERVES ❹

125 g/4 oz/1 cup self-raising flour

pinch of salt

150 ml/¼ pint/⅔ cup milk

1 tbsp melted butter or vegetable oil

1 egg, separated

oil for frying

2 bananas, cut in half lengthways

4 canned pineapple rings, well-drained

1 apple, peeled, cored and cut into 8 rings

75 ml/3 fl oz/⅓ cup plus 1 tbsp golden (light corn) syrup or maple syrup

2 tsp sesame seeds, toasted lightly

1 Sift the flour and salt into a large mixing bowl and make a well in the middle. Pour the milk and melted butter or oil into the well. Add the egg yolk and beat until the batter is smooth. Leave to rest in a cool place for 10 minutes. Just before using, whisk the egg white in a grease-free bowl until stiff, then fold into the batter using a large metal spoon to make it light and airy.

2 Heat the oil in a deep frying-pan (kettle) to a depth of 5 cm/2 inches. Dip the fruit in the batter to give a thin, even coating. Fry in the hot oil, a few pieces at a time, until they are golden brown, turning once. Lift out with a perforated spoon and drain on paper towels. Keep warm while cooking the remaining pieces of fruit.

3 Heat the syrup in a small saucepan. Divide the fritters between 4 hot serving plates and pour the syrup over them. Sprinkle with toasted sesame seeds and serve.

PANCAKES WITH LEMON

Traditionally made as a means of using up flour, eggs and milk before fasting, pancakes are now a well-loved family treat at any time of year.

SERVES 4

125 g/4 oz/1 cup plain (all-purpose) flour

pinch of salt

1 egg

300 ml/½ pint/1¼ cups milk

vegetable oil for frying

caster (superfine) sugar, for sprinkling

lemon wedges to serve

1 Put the flour, salt, egg and milk into a large mixing bowl and beat with a balloon whisk or electric hand mixer to make a smooth batter. Leave to rest for about 10 minutes in a cool place.

2 Heat a heavy-based pancake pan, adding 2–3 drops of oil to grease it, tilting the pan so that the base and sides are

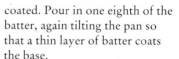

coated. Pour in one eighth of the batter, again tilting the pan so that a thin layer of batter coats the base.

3 Cook over a moderate heat until the base is golden and the batter on the surface has set. Flip over with a palette knife or toss the pancake. Cook until the second side is golden. Turn out on to a warmed plate and keep warm while cooking the rest of the batter, adding 2–3 drops of oil to the pan for each pancake.

Serve sprinkled with sugar and with lemon wedges to squeeze over.

CITRUS SEMOLINA

Milk puddings are quick to make and very nutritious as well as tasty. Try this version of semolina pudding, which is flavoured with the rind and juice of an orange. The sultanas (golden raisins) add texture and sweetness, so very little extra sugar is needed.

SERVES 4

30 g/1 oz/2 tbsp butter or margarine

600 ml/1 pint/2½ cups milk

finely grated rind and juice of 1 large orange

60 g/2 oz/⅓ cup semolina

30 g/1 oz/2 tbsp sugar

30 g/1 oz/3 tbsp sultanas (golden raisins)

1 egg, beaten

pinch of ground nutmeg (freshly ground, if possible)

single (light) cream to serve

1 Grease a 900 ml/1½ pint/ 3½ cup baking dish with a little of the butter or margarine.

2 Put the remaining butter or margarine into a saucepan with the milk and orange rind. Heat gently until the butter has melted, then sprinkle in the semolina, stirring to mix. Bring to the boil, stirring constantly, then reduce the heat and cook for about 2–3 minutes until thickened and smooth. Remove the saucepan from the heat.

3 Stir in the orange juice and sugar, which will cool the mixture slightly, then add the sultanas (golden raisins) and beaten egg, stirring well to mix thoroughly. Transfer to the greased ovenproof dish and sprinkle the surface with the ground nutmeg.

4 Place the dish in a preheated oven at 180°C, 350°F, Gas Mark 4, and bake for 25–30 minutes until the surface of the pudding is golden brown.

HOT LEMON AND LIME SOUFFLE

SERVES ❻

45g/1½ oz/3 tbsp butter

4 tbsp plain (all-purpose) flour

300 ml/½ pint/1¼ cups milk

90 g/3 oz/⅓ cup caster (superfine) sugar

finely grated rind of 1 small lemon

3 tbsp lemon juice

finely grated rind of 1 lime

2 tbsp lime juice

4 eggs, at room temperature, separated

icing (confectioners') sugar for sprinkling

A soufflé is really not difficult to make, but it does need to be eaten the moment it is ready. Don't be tempted to open the oven door to check its progress until towards the end of cooking time, as it could collapse.

1 Grease an 18 cm/7 inch soufflé dish with a little butter.

2 Melt the butter in a saucepan and add the flour. Cook gently for 1 minute. Remove from the heat and add the milk gradually, stirring to mix. Return to the heat and bring to the boil, stirring constantly, until thickened and smooth. Stir in the caster (superfine) sugar, lemon and lime rind and juice. Add the egg yolks and mix well.

3 Whisk the egg whites in a large grease-free bowl until stiff but not dry. Fold into the lemon mixture using a large metal spoon. Pour into the prepared dish.

4 Place on the middle shelf of a preheated oven at 190°C, 375°F, Gas Mark 5, and bake for 25–30 minutes without disturbing, until well risen, golden brown and just

firm to the touch. Serve
immediately, dusted with icing
(confectioners') sugar.

ALMOND BAKED APPLES

Baked apples are full of goodness, and are quick and simple to prepare. In this recipe they are filled with a scrumptious almond and apricot mixture.

1 Grease a shallow ovenproof baking dish with butter. Score the apples around the middle with a sharp knife. Stand them in the baking dish.

2 Mix together the apricots, ground almonds and flaked (slivered) almonds and pack this mixture into the centre of the apples. Put ½ tbsp of the apricot jam (preserves) over the filling and place 15 g/1½ oz/1 tbsp of the butter on top of each apple. Sprinkle with the soft brown sugar and water.

3 Place in a preheated oven at 180°C, 350°F, Gas Mark 4, and bake for about 1 hour, spooning the

syrupy sauce over the apples
occasionally to baste them.

Serve with single (light) cream
or thick natural yogurt.

APPLE AND RAISIN PANCAKES WITH RUM SAUCE

You can prepare this dish in advance by filling the pancakes and making the sauce, then putting both aside until you are ready to bake the pancakes.

SERVES ❹

125 g/4 oz/1 cup plain (all-purpose) flour
1 egg
300 ml/½ pint/1¼ cups milk
vegetable oil for frying
350 g/12 oz cooking apples, peeled, cored and chopped
125 g/4 oz/⅔ cup soft brown sugar
finely grated rind of ½ lemon
2 tbsp lemon juice
30 g/1 oz/3 tbsp raisins or sultanas (golden raisins)
60 g/2 oz/¼ cup butter
2 tbsp golden (light corn) syrup
1 tbsp cornflour (cornstarch)
2 tbsp rum or brandy
150 ml/¼ pint/⅔ cup water

1 Put the flour, egg and milk with a pinch of salt into a large mixing bowl and beat together with a balloon whisk or electric hand mixer to make a smooth batter. Set aside in a cool place to rest for 10 minutes.

2 Heat a heavy-based pancake pan, add 2–3 drops of oil and tilt the pan so that the base and sides are coated. Pour in some batter, tilting the pan so that the batter coats the base. Cook until the base is golden and the top is set, then flip over to cook the other side. Make 8 pancakes, keeping the cooked ones warm.

3 Put the apples, 60 g/2 oz/¼ cup of the sugar, and the lemon rind and juice in a saucepan. Add the raisins and cook until soft. Spoon an equal amount of the mixture on to each pancake, fold into triangles and arrange them in a buttered baking dish.

4 Heat the butter, syrup and remaining sugar gently in a saucepan until the sugar has dissolved. Blend the cornflour (cornstarch) with a little water and add with the rum and the water. Heat, stirring constantly, until thickened and smooth. Pour over the pancakes and bake in a preheated oven at 180°C, 350°F, Gas Mark 4 for 15–20 minutes.

WINTER FRUIT SALAD WITH WHIPPED CREAM

A simmered fruit salad is brought to life with a tot of rum – just the thing for warding off the winter blues.

1 With a potato peeler, pare the rind from the oranges, then peel and segment them, removing all the white pith. Put the rind into a large saucepan with all the other ingredients except for the orange segments, bananas and cream. Cook over a gentle heat until just simmering, then cover and simmer for 10–15 minutes until the plums are tender.

2 Add the orange segments to the pan with the sliced bananas and cook gently for a further 5 minutes. Remove the orange rind and spoon the fruit into 4 serving dishes.

3 Whip the cream until it holds a peak and pile into a small serving bowl. Serve with the hot fruit salad. Natural yogurt also makes a perfect accompaniment, and is lower in calories.

SHERRY AND CINNAMON-SPICED PEARS

A lovely spiced fruit dessert that makes the most of firm, ripe pears. To give it a fabulous finish, whip some fresh cream with a generous pinch of ground cinnamon and spoon on to the hot pears just as you serve them.

1 Cut a tiny slice off the base of each pear to enable it to stand upright. Place the pears in a saucepan and pour in the sherry, water, lemon rind and juice. Add the sugar and cinnamon stick. Place over a gentle heat and simmer for about 10 minutes until the pears are just tender.

2 Lift the pears into serving dishes and pour an equal amount of sherry-flavoured syrup over each.

Whip the cream with the ground cinnamon and serve with the pears.

VANILLA SOUFFLE OMELETTE WITH SUMMER FRUIT FILLING

A sweet soufflé omelette is light and delicious and takes only moments to make. This one is filled with soft summer fruits, dredged with sugar and 'branded' with a hot skewer for the finishing touch.

1 Put the fruit into a saucepan with half the sugar and the wine or apple juice. Simmer gently over a low heat for 2 minutes until the sugar dissolves. Add the blended arrowroot and stir gently until thickened. Remove from the heat.

2 Beat the egg yolks, milk and vanilla flavouring (extract) together. Whisk the egg whites in a large grease-free bowl until stiff but not dry. Add the remaining sugar and whisk for a few more seconds, then fold the egg whites into the egg yolk mixture using a large metal spoon.

3 Melt half the butter in an omelette pan and pour in half the egg mixture. Cook over a medium heat for about 2 minutes to set the base,

then place under a preheated grill (broiler) until the top is set. Turn out on to a warm plate. Quickly make a second omelette with the remaining butter and egg mixture, and turn out on to a second plate.

4 Divide the fruit between the omelettes and fold them over. Dredge them with the icing (confectioners') sugar and 'brand' them with a hot skewer to make a criss-cross pattern.

INDEX